THE SELF HELP BOOK

THE
SELF
HELP
BOOK

6 PRACTICAL WAYS TO
Never Stop Growing

JARED GRAYBEAL

E3

COPYRIGHT © 2020 JARED GRAYBEAL

THE SELF HELP BOOK
6 Practical Ways to Never Stop Growing

ISBN   978-1-5445-1771-1 *Hardcover*

978-1-5445-1770-4 *Paperback*

978-1-5445-1769-8 *Ebook*

For everyone who is prepared to stretch themselves on their leadership journey.

CONTENTS

⁹ *Going on from that place, he went into their synagogue,* ¹⁰ *and a man with a shriveled hand was there. Looking for a reason to bring charges against Jesus, they asked him, "Is it lawful to heal on the Sabbath?"* ¹¹ *He said to them, "If any of you has a sheep and it falls into a pit on the Sabbath, will you not take hold of it and lift it out?* ¹² *How much more valuable is a person than a sheep! Therefore it is lawful to do good on the Sabbath."* ¹³ *Then he said to the man, "**Stretch** out your hand." So he stretched it out and it was completely restored, just as sound as the other.*

—MATTHEW 12:9–13

One hundred percent money-back guarantee if you don't take at least one valuable thing away from this book.

ACKNOWLEDGMENTS

This book is credited first and foremost to God, who gives me the ability to do what I do and stretches me daily. Secondly, to my good friend and brother-from-another-mother, Alex Sanfilippo. He encouraged me, despite my insecurities, that I was a capable writer and asked me to write my first published blog on his website, DailyPS.com. This book wouldn't exist without you always challenging me and my limited understanding of my own abilities. Love you, bro. Also, all my good friends, coworkers, and acquaintances who pushed me along this journey deserve the credit for keeping me going—you know who you are. Lastly, big shout-out to every coffee shop I wrote this in. Below is a list of them:

@southerngrounds

@foxyloxy

@doscoffee

@boldbean

@sagocoffeejax

@cocoandthedirector

NOTE FROM
THE AUTHOR

If you've ever been into exercising, then you probably have heard how important stretching is. Unfortunately, most people don't really know why (which is why most people don't do it). Stretching before and after a workout helps to elongate the muscle, maintain or increase regular blood flow, and not only decrease recovery time but also decrease the risk of injury.

Basically, stretching helps your body stay strong, healthy, and flexible and pushes it to never stop growing.

Just like we need to keep stretching in order to reach

our fitness goals, we have to stretch ourselves in order to reach our personal and professional goals. At least one, if not all six, of the tools discussed in this book will stretch you to a level of discomfort and allow you to stay in a constant season of growth.

My recommendation is: after reading or listening to this book, pick one big thing that stood out to you the most and begin working on it. Once you feel like you have mastered that topic, and if there are others you feel you can grow in, then move on to the next.

INTRODUCTION

SO, WHO AM I, WHY DID I WRITE THIS BOOK, AND WHAT CAN YOU EXPECT?

LET'S START WITH WHO I AM...

My name is Jared Graybeal, and I was born on February 1, 1990, in a really small town in Central Florida called Bartow. I was raised in Lakeland, Florida, which is just a bigger small city next to Bartow (where Publix grocery started).

I'm a NASM Certified Personal Trainer, Fitness Nutrition Specialist, Behavioral Change Specialist, CrossFit Level 2 Trainer, and Corrective Exercise Specialist with an education in marketing and psychology from the University of North Florida.

I own and operate two companies (at this moment but working on a few other projects). One of these is Superfit Foods, a subscription-based, fully customizable healthy prepared food company. The other is E3, a business consulting and marketing agency.

I host a podcast called *The Business and Leadership Podcast*, where I publish monthly, practical teachings on everything business- and leadership-related, and I bring on guest interviewees who are leaders in digital marketing to multimillion-dollar supplement or healthy beverage companies (such as 1st Phorm and FitAid).

I've done a few cool things in my professional life so far, like exhibiting Superfit Foods at Forbes Under 30 and giving a TEDx Talk on nutrition and mental health, and every day I get to work hard at doing what I love.

There is much more to my story, from my complicated upbringing, to my short stint in jail after high school, to a few years on house arrest, to what brought me to my never-ending personal growth journey—but we will cover some of those stories along the way (and most likely in my next book).

Also, as of late, I'm a writer!

I was never good at writing, at least to traditional education standards. I did enough to pass all the English, writing, and literature classes but never felt confident or competent enough to consider myself a writer, or to ever aspire to put anything out in the world.

Until one day I read a quote by Benjamin Franklin that says, "If you would not be forgotten as soon as you are dead and rotten, either write things worth reading or do things worth writing."

Whether it's my own vanity to be known, or a God-given desire to create, this quote inspired me.

Not long after, my good friend Alex Sanfilippo asked me to guest write a blog on his popular Christian blog site, DailyPS.com.

I was nervous, but I felt that if it's for Alex and for his readers, I will put forth the effort. That blog I wrote got a lot of great feedback, so I kept going.

THIS BRINGS ME TO THE NEXT PART: WHY DID I WRITE THIS BOOK?

I've always been passionate about teaching. As a kid, one of my first careers I was interested in was teaching math. After my teachers consistently pointed out that the way I did math was not the way they liked (even though I got the answers right), I decided maybe that wasn't the path for me.

Regardless, everything I learn, I try to teach. I think that's one of the core principles of quality leadership, and I'm grateful that it has always come so natural to me.

Once I began writing blogs, I realized that I had sort of been doing this my whole adult life. From the time I was nineteen and managing health-club chains and creating training documents, until now, I've been writing blog-like teachings on a regular basis. I just never thought of it that way.

As I transitioned out of the corporate world and into owning my own businesses, I carried that same habit of teaching. I would write my teachings ahead of time in a blog format, so it was much easier to memorize or at least use for notes as I taught.

When my business started to grow and I became more recognized, I began getting asked to teach and speak publicly. One of those opportunities was at a church I was involved in, and that's when I began writing content for a four-part teaching called "Taming the Lion: The Biblical and Ethical Principles of Leadership and Entrepreneurship."

My ultimate goal was to write a book from this teaching, so I started. But I really had no idea what I was doing. After about a year, I took a break from writing the book.

During my break, I was inspired to write another blog that I wanted to use as a teaching for my podcast, and it was called "6 Practical Ways to Never Stop Growing."

Well, I got so into this blog that it ended up being about ten thousand words. My podcasts are intended to be commute-worthy fifteen- to twenty-minute teachings, and this would have been much longer than that. Knowing that I had left stuff out with the intention of keeping it short, I decided then that I would revisit that blog, put everything

I had into it, and that would be my first book. And here we are!

My mission in life is to encourage, educate, and empower others to live happier, healthier lives—and every piece of content I put out, this book largely included, is my practical way of accomplishing that mission. I hope this book does exactly that.

Maybe, at the time you're reading this, my second book has already come out—*Taming the Lion*. If so, I highly recommend you check it out at some point.

LASTLY, WHAT CAN YOU EXPECT FROM READING THIS BOOK?

I write in such a way that coincides with how my brain works. In order for me to absorb content, it has to be practical, informational, and realistic. Additionally, some stories, steps, and examples really help me.

Those are things you can look forward to as you read. This book was intended to be short enough to give you the information you need with some supportive and hopefully entertaining stories or examples, and nothing more. I'm not a big fan of two-hundred-page books with a ton of fluff just to reach their page-count goal from their publicist when it really could have been 110 pages and I would have gotten the point. So, I promise, I only kept what I felt was necessary in this book in order for you to understand each concept and be able to take action on them.

Personal growth is a never-ending journey, which means at any time throughout your life, you will be able to reference this book and most likely identify an area where you once again need to grow.

With that being said, I recommend reading this book once a year, which is another reason why I kept it short.

LET'S GET INTO IT

Have you ever felt stuck? Like you've been doing the same routine forever, and you're not growing in any way? Well, you're not alone.

A study of two thousand people found that 69 percent feel trapped in the same old routine and over

40 percent are generally unhappy with their lives because of it.[1]

In this book, I'm going to outline the three main reasons that people get stuck in the first place, give you the six ways to get unstuck, and give you practical examples of your next steps so you can live a life of endless personal growth. But first, why is "getting unstuck" even that important? Especially if you're comfortable there...

According to Bronnie Ware, a palliative-care nurse, the greatest regret people had when they were on their death bed was, "I wish I'd had the courage to live a life true to myself, not the life others expected of me."

She goes on to write:

> "This was the most common regret of all. When people realize that their life is almost over and look back clearly on it, it is easy to see how many dreams have gone unfulfilled. Many people had not honored even a half of their dreams and had to die knowing that it was due to choices they had made, or not made."[2]

The goal here is to not wait until our last days to realize our potential and regret the way we lived our lives. God has created each and every one for some form of greatness, whether it's to be the best third-grade teacher possible, the quickest and most accurate delivery driver, or the next president of the United States—in any case, it's our responsibility to find that out and figure out how to get there.

CHAPTER 1

THE 5 MAIN REASONS WHY PEOPLE GET STUCK

Before teaching on all the ways to never stop growing, I wanted to make sure we cover the reasons why we get stuck in the first place. Without first acknowledging some of the things that hold us back, we may never have the humility and maturity to approach the 6 Ways with the right mindset.

REASON #1: WE STOP LEARNING.

"Life is like riding a bicycle. To keep your balance, you must keep moving."

—ALBERT EINSTEIN

Unfortunately, after we finish school and get a job, most people stop deliberately trying to learn. It could be because of burnout from the education system, or it could simply be because committing to a life of never-ending learning is hard. There are a lot of easier and more immediately rewarding things to do with our time after we get off work, like watching TV, scrolling on social media, or hanging out with friends. Unless you're forced to learn things at work in order to keep your job, most people don't commit to a life of continued education.

REASON #2: WE DON'T SET GOALS.

According to the latest research, less than 3 percent of Americans have written goals, and less than 1 percent review and rewrite their goals on a daily basis.[3]

Why?

LACK OF SELF-CONFIDENCE

Our internal dialogue is most often more pessimistic than optimistic, and especially when trying something new, we have no past successes to reflect on. It can be extremely hard to recruit the confidence you need to move forward on a path you've never taken. This book is going to go over how to grow in that area.

FEAR OF FAILURE

Our fear of failure is ultimately rooted in pride. Most of us, aside from the fear of losing money from a failure, aren't really afraid of failure. We are afraid of other people *seeing* us fail. Our ego can be very empowering, but it can also be extremely limiting.

LAZINESS AND COMFORT

Setting goals and pursuing growth requires a lot of work, and some people are simply not ambitious enough to step outside of their comfort zone and put in the work to get to the next level.

IMPATIENCE

We live in a world of instant gratification. With almost everything at our fingertips, we expect personal growth to be the same. As they say, "If it was easy, everyone would be doing it." In order to see continued growth over time, it is much like the investment game. Accrued interest over time can amount to a lot of money, but you have to be patient.

REASON #3: WHEN WE DO SET GOALS, WE SUCK AT IT.

Studies show that less than 25 percent of us actually stick to New Year's resolutions after thirty days, and only 8 percent accomplish them. Clearly, there's something wrong with how we are setting goals.

Why?

Because most of us just don't know how. Brian Tracy, self-development author and goal-setting expert, says, "One of the greatest tragedies of our educational system is that you can receive fifteen to eighteen years of education in our schools and never once receive a single hour of instruction on how to set goals."

REASON #4: WE ARE TOO ONE-TRACK-MINDED ABOUT GROWTH.

Most people think growth is linear, assuming you can only grow in one way at one time. Then they get stuck on it.

For example, if you're trying to get a promotion, you dial into the lifestyle it takes to get that promotion and forsake everything else. Or if you're trying to lose weight, you do a mediocre job at work, maybe hang with your friends when it's convenient, but give your fitness goals 100 percent of your attention.

The problem with this is that we stay there, and even once we've reached our goal, we don't think to diversify until we've sunk into the depressive state of being stuck again.

REASON #5: GROWTH CAN BE PAINFUL.

When I was in high school, I was 4'11" until my junior year. I prayed daily to grow, but nothing happened...until eleventh grade. I grew seven inches that year (and about three inches more since then, thankfully), and I can remember how painful that was. Seven inches in one year is an unusual growth spurt, and it caused a lot of pain to my joints, especially my hips. But as I was going through that pain, I was also very thankful, because I had gotten the growth I had been praying for.

Personal growth can be much like that. Both the work required and the change that comes with the results can be painful at times, and some people aren't cut out for that level of discomfort.

Once you accept that pain is a part of growth, you will also be able to enjoy the fruits of it later on and live a life of constant, positive change.

Now that we've covered the bad news and the not-so-fun statistics, here's the good news: **you can change**.

Getting unstuck isn't that hard—I promise. It's just a few small, simple steps done consistently over time. You can live a life of greatness, fulfill your potential, and be happy doing it. Most importantly, you can start right now.

Not next Monday, next month, or next January.

RIGHT NOW.

Now that we're fully committed to the growth journey, and we've accepted that in the past we may have given up, stopped learning, or at least set goals the wrong way, it's time to change that—with one of the best ways I know how: building your confidence.

CHAPTER 2

CONFIDENCE

"With realization of one's own potential and self-confidence in one's ability, one can build a better world."

—DALAI LAMA

HOW DO WE CONSISTENTLY GROW IN OUR CONFIDENCE?

Well, first off, how do we know if we need to grow in our confidence?

Self-confidence can be defined as a belief in one's abilities and maintaining a sense of competence. On the other hand, low self-confidence can be defined as a lack of faith in one's abilities and competence.

Self-confidence can fuel success, while low self-esteem can impede it. To avoid falling into patterns of low self-esteem and a lack of confidence, ask yourself the following questions:

Maybe take out a notebook and write your answers down, or use the blank space, so you can have your responses for later reference.

1. Are you always comparing yourself to others? When that happens, do you feel better, or worse?

2. Do you set goals? If you do, are they relatively challenging? If you don't, think about why.

3. How do you respond when someone gives you a compliment?

4. Do you ever find yourself seeking validation in ways that are antithetical to your personal values?

5. How do you feel when you get all dressed up, go out, and don't get the compliments you were expecting?

6. Would you consider yourself an "assertive" person?

7. How often do you contribute your own opinion or perspective during conversations with friends, family, or coworkers?

8. How well do you take constructive criticism?

9. Are you the type of person to back down during a disagreement, despite your beliefs?

10. Are you always on your phone in public settings like parties, meetings, networking events, etc.?

11. On a scale of one to ten, how excited are you for the future?

12. Do you trust yourself?

TIP #1: CHANGE YOUR SELF-TALK.

This is a big one and can be pretty challenging, depending on how your current relationship with self-talk is. Before we commit to changing our self-talk, we need to understand what it is.

Self-talk, also known as internal monologue, is a person's inner voice that provides a running verbal monologue of thoughts while that person is conscious. It is usually tied to your sense of self. It is crucial to planning, problem solving, self-reflection, self-image, critical thinking,[4] and emotions.[5]

WHAT IS NEGATIVE SELF-TALK?

There are a few different types of negative self-talk. Some are just common sense, such as "This pan is hot, so I shouldn't touch it." The other kind, which is the kind I'm referencing, is the kind that just beats you up inside.

For example, saying, "I'm a crappy writer." Just because you got a C on a test in literature in college years ago does not mean you are actually a bad writer. It might mean that you didn't follow all the rules, and maybe you need some work, but you aren't a "crappy" writer.

I used to tell myself this all of the time. I was good at speaking, great at showing people examples, but I just couldn't put my words into writing in a way that I felt good about.

Why? Because I got mediocre English grades in school and a bad grade in literature class in college, I was convinced that I was bad at writing. Since reframing my self-talk and building my confidence in this area, I've written countless blogs, training manuals for some of the largest health clubs in the country, and this book you are now reading (hopefully it's good so far!).

The echoes of your negative self-talk, or "inner critic," may sound a lot like a critical parent, a not-so-great friend, or a crazy ex that you dated for too long—from your past. It can follow the path of typical cognitive distortions, which is simply when your mind convinces you of something that isn't true. Basically, negative self-talk is any inner dialogue you have with yourself that may be limiting your ability to believe in yourself and your own abilities to reach your potential. It is any thought that diminishes you and your ability to make positive changes in your life or your confidence in your ability to do so. Because of this, negative self-talk can not only be stressful, but can really stunt your leadership potential.[6]

CONSEQUENCES OF NEGATIVE SELF-TALK

Our perception is most often our reality, so what we think will eventually manifest itself in some pretty unhealthy ways. Studies have linked negative self-talk with:

- Lower self-esteem

- Higher levels of stress

- Decreased motivation

- Greater feelings of helplessness

- Depression

- Relationship challenges

If you find yourself actively engaging in this type of dialogue with yourself, then you know the feeling. Negativity is a self-deprecating cycle that can make progress and reaching the goals you set for yourself very difficult.

NOW THAT WE KNOW WHAT IT IS AND WHY IT'S BAD, WHAT DO WE DO ABOUT IT?

Shift to positive self-talk. Just like negative-self talk is a predictor of complacency, positive self-talk has an effect on your reality, making it much easier to reach your goals and grow as a leader.

For example, one study on athletes compared four different types of self-talk (**instructional**: where athletes remind themselves of specific things to do to play better; **motivational**: self-talk that keeps people on-task; **positive**; and **negative**) and found that positive self-talk was the greatest predictor of success. People didn't need to remind themselves how to do something as much as they needed to tell themselves that they are doing something great and that others notice it as well.[7]

FOUR STEPS TO SHIFT FROM NEGATIVE TO POSITIVE SELF-TALK

Once you commit to changing your self-talk from negative to positive, you have to start paying more attention to yourself. When you begin to recognize moments where you internalize negative self-talk or say it out loud, you have to catch yourself in that moment and reframe it.[8] Just like the times your dog pees in the house, you have to let them know what they did wrong right away. If you wait until tomorrow, they won't be able to associate the punishment with the crime.[9] When it comes to recognizing and changing habits, humans aren't much different.

STEP 1: JOURNALING

Whether you want to carry a journal around with you during the day and jot down negative comments when you think them, or write consistently at the beginning or end of the day, journaling can be an effective tool for examining your inner process.

STEP 2: THINK LIKE A (GOOD) FRIEND

Some of the things we tell ourselves, we would NEVER say to other people. Especially our good friends, even when we're being brutally honest. That's because some of the things we tell ourselves simply aren't true. Next time you have a negative thought about yourself, just ask, "Would I say this to a good friend, or would a good friend of mine say this to me?"

STEP 3: USE THE RUBBER-BAND TRICK

I learned this in therapy at a young age. I think I remember my therapist asking me to try this trick in order to help me stop biting my nails or saying mean things. Safe to say, I was somewhat of a troubled kid, but it definitely helped! Anytime I'd catch myself biting my nails or saying something mean, I'd pull the rubber band back and let it snap. It caused a little pain, but it created a negative association and an unfavorable consequence for those actions, which made me want to do it less and less over time.

STEP 4: REALISTIC REFRAMING

Reframing is a technique used in therapy to help create a different way to look at something, and in this instance, we are going to reframe your potentially negative perspective to a more realistic one. Positive self-talk still requires that you are somewhat realistic in your approach. It's not intended to convince you that you can go run a marathon when you haven't exercised in three months. By using realistic reframing, you will convince the more analytical part of your brain of what you are really capable of.

EXAMPLE

Instead of "I'm a bad test taker," you would say to yourself, "In the past, I have had a harder time than most people with tests, so in order to do well on this next test, I just need to find alternative ways to study to make sure I remember the content. I'm a smart person, and I always remember this stuff when it comes to real-life situations, so I'm sure I can find a way to remember it for a test."

Key points in this example:

- You recognized what the former version of you has struggled with.

- You acknowledged that you, like everyone else, have the power to change, grow, and get better at things.

- You realistically approached a solution to a problem you have experienced in the past.

- You affirmed your capabilities in order to reinforce your new solution.

Doing this won't change everything in your life right away, but after creating a habit of reframing your negative self-talk to something more positive and realistic, in time you will do this without thinking about it. You'll be a completely different person—in the best way.

How we talk to ourselves makes a huge impact on our confidence, but there are other ways to grow in this area as well. Let's explore some more.

TIP #2: GROOM YOURSELF.

"If you look good, you feel good. If you feel good, you play good. If you play good, they pay good."

—DEION SANDERS

This may seem like a given, but when people struggle with confidence, sometimes they fail to recognize the obvious. Start with the basics, like hygiene, then move on to things like your outfits and hair. Here are six recommendations—in order of importance.

1. KEEP YOUR TEETH HEALTHY.

According to a study from the University of Leeds featured on Business Insider, clean white teeth are a quick indicator of good health and thus instantly make us more attractive to others.[10]

- Brush two to three times per day.

- Floss daily.

- Find a good dentist and get regular checkups, cleanings, and whitening (shout-out, Dr. Pauline!).

Growing up, like most kids, I reluctantly brushed my teeth once a day. As I got older and began to be more conscious of my looks (not necessarily my health), I would brush twice a day every so often. I also didn't have health insurance, so that was a good motivator for me to take care of my teeth.

When I was nineteen and got promoted to my first management role in the health club I was working at, I finally got health insurance. I visited the dentist right away, and basically got scared straight. Because I never flossed, never saw a dentist, and usually only brushed once a day, I had a ton of bacteria built up in my gums, and the dentist quoted me eight thousand dollars to do a "deep clean" in order to avoid gingivitis.

When I left, I called my friend's mom, whose husband was a dentist. I called to ask her what she thought about that price and if I should do it, and she recommended I see a different dentist, who charged me $80 and took great care of me.

I got lucky, but I learned that by not brushing two or three times a day, and never flossing, bacteria builds up. For one, it's super gross and can make your breath smell bad. Secondly and most importantly, that bacteria that builds up in your mouth from neglecting your hygiene can eventually cause negative effects in your brain and your digestive system.[11] Spending ten minutes out of your twenty-four hours in the day on this one thing could dramatically increase your confidence and your health and, in turn, create a multiplier effect on your day-to-day outcomes.

2. WEAR DEODORANT (MAYBE GET A NEW KIND IF YOU NOTICE YOURSELF HALFWAY THROUGH THE DAY SMELLING LIKE YOU ALREADY WORKED OUT).

We all know that one person who, either toward the end of the workday, or during a workout, just smells like BO (body odor). Don't be that person. Understandably, hormones and other factors can affect this, which is why you need to make sure to find a product that works for you and don't just stick with the same thing you have used since you were a kid.

I actually have a friend whom I recently went on a trip with, and we got caught up in a conversation about wearing cologne and deodorant. It turns out, his wife sleeps really oddly with her hands behind her head, and in the middle of the night, he always wakes up to the stench of her armpits. Neither of them knew why, and she began wearing male deodorant before going to bed in hopes to avoid the stench and waking him up.

I asked her if she has nightmares, and she said she does, regularly. Which made me think about myself. I struggle with anxiety from time to time, and when it's bad, my armpits will run straight through my deodorant. It's the weirdest thing. So I did some research and found that heightened levels of anxiety can actually cause an increase in the odor of your perspiration.[12]

I say all that just to reiterate the importance of knowing yourself well and knowing how to be prepared. Although I can't necessarily teach in depth on avoiding anxiety or nightmares, I can tell you how I prepare. I simply always have an extra stick of deodorant in my truck, office, and gym bag just in case those higher-level-stress days come about. If I didn't have that on me when heading to a meeting, then I'd be self-conscious and insecure the whole time.

3. HAVE A QUICK NIGHTTIME HYGIENE ROUTINE WHERE YOU CARE FOR YOUR SKIN (FACE AND BODY) AND THE SMALL THINGS MOST PEOPLE (ESPECIALLY GUYS) DON'T THINK ABOUT, LIKE FINGERNAILS, TOENAILS, NOSTRIL HAIRS, UNIBROWS, ETC.

This isn't just about how you look; it's also about how you feel. A regular nighttime routine helps your body and mind recognize that it's bedtime, which leads to better sleep and ultimately a better day.[13]

I'm not a big skin-care influencer, so I don't have many insights on the topic. I do know that when coming up with your nighttime skincare routine, it's important to consider your lifestyle and to see a dermatologist.

By consulting a professional and considering the type of life that you live, it will help you decide if you need a simple or complex routine, and if there are any particular products that you might favor. I'm a simple dude, so my routine is pretty simple. I splash my face with cold water, use a cleanser, and then wash it off with cold water. Then before I go to bed, I put lotion on. Even though it's simple, it goes a long way in managing my oily face and the dryness on my body from being in the Florida sun so often.

As far as the remaining small items like nails and nostril hairs, just take a close look in the mirror and you'll know what you need to do.

4. ALWAYS HAVE A LIGHT COAT OF A HIGHLY RATED COLOGNE OR PERFUME ON. NOT TOO MUCH BUT NOT TOO LITTLE—AND KEEP IT IN THE CAR IF YOU FEEL LIKE IT WEARS OFF QUICKLY.

It never hurts to be the person who's known to always smell good. It does hurt, however, to be known as the person who wears too much cologne or perfume. And if no one ever compliments you on how you smell, assuming you don't wear anything, then it's not like you're losing—you're just not winning.

In high school, when I really started caring about what others (mainly girls) think, I decided to invest in some cologne. I say "invest" because this was coming out of my own pocket. And as a sixteen-year-old, living on my own and barely getting by, a sixty-dollar bottle of cologne was an investment.

Everyone I knew was wearing Acqua Di Gio, and it smelled great. But I didn't want to smell like everyone. I still wanted to smell good, so I visited a cologne store with a girl I knew, and with her help, I found something that smelled equally as good, but just not the same. I have literally been wearing Polo Black ever since, and I get compliments all the time. That little compliment, every once in a while, might just be the one boost of confidence I need to close the next deal or establish the next partnership. Little stuff like that goes a long way, so give it a try.

5. TAKE THE TIME TO ESTABLISH A FEW OUTFIT ROTATIONS THAT YOU'VE NOTICED IN THE PAST LOOK GOOD AND IN WHICH YOU FEEL CONFIDENT.

New research out of Princeton University finds that we determine people's competence within seconds partially by the subtle economic cues tied to their clothing.[14] You have to take this within context, because for the well-known leaders, entrepreneurs, celebrities, and influencers in the world, this may not necessarily apply. That's because they have already established themselves as a master of their craft in their field, and Elon Musk is okay to wear sweatpants to a meeting without being judged as incompetent. But the rest of us, until we become known as experts in our field or in the general public, this study applies.

Long story short—the term "dress to impress" still stands, and it's worth the time to choose ahead of time a few outfits you feel confident in and put those in your weekly rotation. If you take a look at your wardrobe and realize you need to upgrade, then I guarantee it's worth the investment. If you have outgrown your favorite clothes or have lost weight, it's time to make an investment in a few new items so you can feel good about what you wear in public.

There are so many online clothing companies that will send you clothes to try, and if you don't like them, you can send them back. Shopping for clothes and looking your best has never been so easy, so take the time and watch your confidence increase.

P.S. Make sure to donate the clothes that you don't wear anymore!

6. IDENTIFY WHAT KIND OF HAIR YOU FEEL BEST IN, AND MAKE SURE YOU WAKE UP EARLY ENOUGH IN THE MORNING TO GET IT TO LOOK THAT WAY BEFORE YOU START YOUR DAY.

A little more sleep always sounds good in the moment, but when you get to the office and realize you're presenting a proposal to the big wigs that day, you'll wish you would have spent that time getting ready.

This is much like the previous point. Unless you've established yourself as a pro in your field or some type of celeb, it's important to be presentable. I see a lot of (mainly young) people showing up to work with messy hair, as if "not caring" is cool. Unless that's your culture, then in my opinion, it's unacceptable.

This may not apply to everyone, but I know that when I'm a few days overdue for a haircut, it affects my confidence. Knowing that, I schedule a haircut every two weeks like clockwork. These days, you never know when you'll end up in a public picture or video, and the last thing you want is to be having a bad hair day.

TIP #3: SET SMALL GOALS—AND MAKE SURE TO ACCOMPLISH THEM.

My recommendation when goal-setting in the beginning is always the same, and I will repeat this a few times throughout the book: set SMART goals.[15]

Specific—Your goal is direct, detailed, and meaningful. Not vague and irrelevant.

Measurable—Your goal is quantifiable to track progress along the way or success.

Attainable—Your goal is realistic, and you have the tools or the resources in order to accomplish it.

Relevant—Your goal aligns with your vision of your future for your life and your personal values.

Time-based—Your goal has a deadline. It can't just happen whenever.

Apply this technique and set a few small goals that can be reached on a daily or weekly basis. Most people make the mistake of setting too big of goals. Setting big goals is the ultimate destination, but before we get there, ya gotta start small. Consistently accomplishing goals, no matter the size, will inevitably increase your confidence in yourself.

- Want to get in shape and lose twenty pounds? Start by losing one pound.

  One pound is 3,500 calories. So to lose one pound of fat, you need to either burn 3,500 calories, eat 3,500 fewer calories, or find a happy medium—depending on your lifestyle and what got you "overweight" in the first place.

  This is just a general example, so don't necessarily take this as a prescription for yourself. But to lose one pound in one week, you need a 3,500-calorie deficit.

  3,500/7=500 calories per day

  You could exercise to burn three hundred more calories a day, and eat two hundred calories less per day, and reach that goal.

- Want to start dating, but you're uncomfortable with asking people out in fear of failure? Start by meeting one person.

This simply comes down to the "Law of Large Numbers."[16] The more people you meet, the more likely you'll meet someone whom you are interested in and who is equally interested in you.

You just have to stop psyching yourself out by thinking too much into it. Stop thinking about asking someone out, and just set a goal to meet them. You can't fail at meeting someone.

Most people are awake about seventeen hours per day, and in public half that time. That's eight and a half hours every day that you have a chance to meet someone new. Whether it's at work, in the gym, at the grocery store, or at the dog park, start with a handshake, ask for a name, give them yours, and ask a genuine question. It's that simple.

- Want to start reading books but never considered yourself a "reader?" Find a book you

KNOW you will like (read reviews), and commit to reading five pages a day.

This doesn't even have to be a self-help book (like this one, which I made short for this exact reason), a finance book, or a business book. It could be Harry Potter. Just find a book that you know you'll like, and by reading a few pages of that each day, you will build a habit of reading every day, which will eventually translate into a discipline that you can carry over to those more "productive" books that will make you better at your work or craft.

- Want to be more productive throughout the day but have a hard time joining the five o'clock or six o'clock in the morning club? Start by waking up fifteen minutes earlier for a few weeks.

Week 1:

If you normally get up at half past eight o'clock in the morning, start this week off by getting up at a quarter past eight o'clock in the morning. Do that every day this week, at least for the weekdays.

Week 2:

Now get up at eight o'clock in the morning every day.

Week 3:

A quarter 'til eight o'clock in the morning.

You get the drift...

Keep in mind, waking up at five o'clock or six o'clock in the morning only makes sense if that's what you need to do to accomplish your goals. It has to be relevant. You can't do it just because some people you follow on Instagram do. I have a friend that is up at four o'clock in the morning every day, and it works perfectly for him. I recently saw that Mark Wahlberg apparently gets up at a quarter 'til three o'clock in the morning every day. Personally, I'm out of bed by half past six o'clock in the morning every day, and that's what works for me. Find your time, and inch your way each week with those fifteen-minute intervals until you get there.

TIP #4: SMILE MORE.

This is simple and effective, especially if you have put into practice all the preceding steps. When you smile at another person, the physical action releases endorphins in your brain. Endorphins are nature's "happy drug." They make you feel happy and raise your self-esteem. When you smile, you feel and act in a more personable way to everyone around you and you give off confidence.[17]

TIP #5: TAKE A STEP FORWARD.

You have to flex your risk-taking muscle in order to increase your confidence. Yes, you will fail more— that is the inevitable result of trying harder. But the most confident people you know are the ones who set their pride aside and simply try harder, and more often. So ask the girl (or guy) out, send that resume in and make the phone call to follow up, or sign up for that half marathon. Whatever it is, start going for it more often!

As you can tell from reading this far, acquiring or increasing your self-confidence doesn't have to come from worldly things like more likes on social media or more followers—it can and will come from practical things, like working on how well you take care of yourself, both inside and out.

In this next chapter, we are going to cover one of the greatest gifts that, when nurtured, will always keep on giving. This next one has changed my life in so many ways that it couldn't possibly all fit in this book.

CHAPTER 3

CONNECTIONS

"You can make more friends in two months by becoming interested in other people than you can in two years by trying to get other people interested in you."

—DALE CARNEGIE, *HOW TO WIN FRIENDS AND INFLUENCE PEOPLE*

Any success I have is a product of the connections I've been blessed to create over the years. My dad was a very social person, and one thing he taught me that I will never forget is the value of connections and always showing everyone love. Growing up, we didn't have much. My dad struggled to raise me and my brother on his own with an independent contracting job, and we were always bouncing from place to place. I watched how my dad always leveraged his connections to get us by, and anyone he ever encountered appreciated his presence. Whether it was leveraging his friendships to get him part-time work to cover the bills, or needing a place for us to stay for a few nights, my dad always had someone he could lean on. He was a loving and appreciative guy, so this part came natural to me.

Since I was young, I was never particularly gifted in any area that would draw people to me. I wasn't very good at sports, and I didn't have much to offer, but I naturally valued connections and treated the people close to me as good as I could. I've always been open-minded to meeting more people. Neither one of my businesses would exist if I hadn't been open to grabbing coffee with a stranger from time to time.

This book wouldn't even exist if I hadn't overcome the discomfort of visiting an awkward church group and meeting Alex Sanfillipo, who has become one of my best friends.

So sometimes...the best way to stretch yourself when you're feeling stuck is to expand your connections.

Let's kick off this chapter with a few more questions—just so we can measure the potential value of adding some connections in our life:

1. When was the last time you met someone new?

2. Who is a connection you made that, without your realizing it, has massively changed your life? How did you meet this person?

3. What goals do you have right now that would be easier if you had help from a new connection that you don't have now?

HOW DO WE GROW IN THE AREA OF OUR CONNECTIONS?

These are literally going to be the most practical ways to meet new people.

TIP #1: JOIN A GROUP, OR EVEN A NETWORKING GATHERING RELEVANT TO YOUR CAREER.

I make the mistake all the time of expecting new connections to just pop up on my radar, without putting forth any effort. But when you take inventory and realize that you might be at a connection deficit, then it's time to do the work. This can be much easier than you think. All you have to do is take a few minutes on the internet and look up the following:

LOCAL BNI GROUPS

What is BNI?

Business Network International. Members meet weekly to discuss business and support each other's businesses by sharing referrals. It claims to be the world's leading "referral organization."[18]

Searching this will most likely direct you to www.bni.com. From here, you are going to put in your area code. When I did this, twenty-five different groups within fifteen miles of me popped up.

LOCAL ROTARY CLUBS (OR ROTARACT IF YOU'RE A YOUNG ADULT)

What is a Rotary?

Rotary International is an international service

organization whose stated purpose is to bring together business and professional leaders in order to provide humanitarian service and to advance goodwill and peace around the world.[19]

Searching this will most likely direct you to www.rotary.org. Once you're on that page, click "Club Finder." From there, you will enter your area information. When I put my city in, I found twelve clubs within twenty-five miles that meet weekly.

CHURCH COMMUNITY GROUPS

If you go to church, this is an excellent way to meet people. If you're new to a city, and assuming you're a believer, I highly recommend that one of the first things you do is find a "home church." It's hard to create community if you're always church-hopping.

Once you've established a church as where you will regularly attend, I am sure that their website will have information on groups. Personally, I've only been to a few groups that I liked. But I had to go to a lot in order to find myself in one with like-minded people.

Since I value community so much, I ended up starting two groups of my own. I now lead a biweekly men's Bible study group at my house, and a monthly group called "Faith and Fitness," where we meet at the beach or a local gym, I teach a short devotional, and I create a workout that typically lasts about twenty minutes.

What is really cool is that this group is typically two-thirds Christians and one-third non-believers or people who aren't sure about their faith. I have seen some really cool things happen since starting these groups, and they have created some of the best relationships I have in my life to this day.

Whether it's joining a group or starting your own, this is an excellent way to stretch your connections' muscle. If you want to hear more about how I started my own, feel free to reach out to me on Instagram or via email.

EVENTBRITE EVENTS

Most people don't know about this one. Once you search this, you will most likely see the link to www.eventbrite.com. From there, click "Discover Events." If your computer has you geotagged, it will pop up with events in your area. If not, you will have to input your area. Once you do, a plethora of different-themed events from home-buying to bar crawls will pop up.

Be open-minded, grab a friend, and go check one of these out. Tell them you were inspired by this book to do it, and then convince them to buy themselves a copy!

DOWNLOAD THE "MEETUP" APP (OR VISIT THE WEBSITE)

This is really cool. Once you visit the app/site, you will see that there are meetups for board games, hiking, marathon training, learning to cook, and practicing a new language. I highly recommend checking it out if you're not into the traditional networking settings.

FACEBOOK GROUPS

This is basically Facebook's version of Meetup. If you're already on Facebook, it's convenient because you can invite friends and tag friends to see if they're interested, and it's all on one platform that you are probably already using.

TIP #2: LEVERAGE SOCIAL MEDIA TO TALK MORE ABOUT WHAT YOU DO.

This can be huge for you! And for most people, it's severely underutilized. Most people spend too much time browsing social media, or what I call "taking." If you are going to use the platform, then you at least need to have a fifty/fifty (at a bare minimum) ratio of giving and taking. Meaning, you need to be putting out valuable content regularly if you are using the platform regularly.

For example, let's say you are on social media two hours per day (which is actually below average). In my opinion, and what I am proposing, is that one hour out of that time should be spent posting valuable content. Whether it's a picture with text on Instagram, or sharing your thoughts or a quote you read on Facebook, we have a responsibility to contribute if we are going to take so much. Even if it's posting a funny meme, you are providing value to people who look for that stuff to brighten their day.

The positive result behind this is that like-minded people will begin to gravitate toward your page and, ultimately, to you. If you take advantage of these opportunities, you can expand your network in a life-changing way. Some of my best friends and mentors came from social media connections.

Two years ago, a dude saw my Instagram page because a mutual friend of ours shared a post of mine. Because he checked out my page and saw that we shared a lot of the same values (fitness, faith, leadership, personal growth, etc.), he reached out. Ten years ago, this would have been weird, but we DM'd a bit and planned a meetup when he came to my city for business. Since then, we have grown to be best friends. He is one of two guys I reach out to in my darkest moments, and he's the first or second to hear about the great things that happen in my life. All because I share about my passions, my values, my goals, and myself on my social platforms.

TIP #3: MAKE A CONSCIOUS EFFORT TO MEET MORE PEOPLE.

I talked a little bit about this when I mentioned setting small goals, but it applies just as much here when making an intentional effort to simply create new connections. If you are like most people, you probably get coffee at a coffee shop, you might go to a local gym, you might be in school, or you might work for a large company where new people are coming and going all the time. These are all opportunities to most likely meet one new person every day. After enough days of stepping outside of your comfort zone and introducing yourself to new people, you are bound to organically create a new connection that can help you get to the next level.

Personally, I have a list of fifteen things I try to do every single day. One of those things is "meet someone new." When I do, I try to learn one thing about them, so that afterward, I can write down their name and what I learned about them in my phone. That might sound excessive, but it's really come in handy over time.

I'm biased, though, because I'm somewhat of an extrovert. I understand that for introverts, meeting people doesn't come as easily and putting yourself out there can take a lot of emotional energy.

With that being said, here are four tips for places that introverts can meet people more easily, and how to go about doing so without being super awkward:

1. Go to the gym—For this particular tip, I'm referring to a health-club-style gym. If you're the type who likes to exercise alone, then this is where you want to start. Next time you attempt a challenging lift, like bench press or shoulder press, where it's reasonable to have a spotter, ask a stranger to spot you. From there, thank them for their help and introduce yourself. The conversation should take off from there.

2. Join a group training gym—Like CrossFit, Orange Theory, or Cycle Bar. One of the great benefits of group training gyms is their culture. Typically, the trainer will introduce you to the class anyway, since it'll be your first time. After doing a few workouts, it's inevitable to have met a handful of the people who go there. If you decide to stick to a certain time, then you'll be a part of that group in no time.

3. The coffee shop—There are a few different ways to meet someone at the coffee shop. If you're brand new to the idea of meeting new people, then start with the barista. Order your drink, then say, "Hey, I'm Jared, by the way. What's your name?" After doing that, you'll gain a bit

of confidence. Once you're sitting down, drinking your coffee and getting your work done, just pay attention to your surroundings. You will see people reading books, doing homework, studying, or having conversations. Use your common sense here. You never want to use eavesdropping as an intro, but if you see someone working on homework and the book is from a local college, spark up a quick conversation about their class or that school. In these settings, you always want to keep the subject matter of the conversation light, so you aren't pulling them too far from what they were doing. Once you've exchanged a few sentences, give them your name, ask them theirs, then go back to what you were doing. You might get lucky and this turns into a full conversation, or at the least, you will see them again and now you know them!

4. The dog park (assuming you have a dog)—There are really two main ways to meet people at the dog park. Let your dog run up on them, then apologize, and introduce yourself. Or you can ask people what kind of dog they have (unless it's super obvious), then compliment them

on how cool their dog looks or how well it's behaved, then introduce yourself.

TIP #4: SERVE/VOLUNTEER.

Regardless of your ambitions, regularly committing to serving, in some capacity, is just good human practice and it's good for your soul. Altruistic motives aside, it can be an additional way to meet some great new people. I'm sure if you Googled "local volunteer opportunities," you would find plenty, but here are a few examples:

SERVE AT YOUR LOCAL CHURCH (GREETING, USHERING, PARKING, CREATIVE, WORSHIP TEAM, ETC.)

When I first began my "faith journey," I knew I had to transition the environments I was spending my time in in order to live a different lifestyle, but I didn't have many Christian friends. I was going to church every week, and they would always mention serving opportunities. Of course, at first, I was hesitant. The commitment, the time, the new people... it all gave me anxiety. But once I just showed up to the first huddle and did my orientation to start greeting people at the front doors, it was all down-hill from there.

I met a bunch of great people. Some of the connections I established have brought me in to speak to their organizations, some have become close friends of mine, and some have become people I've been able to contribute to through my life experiences and the things I've learned. All very valuable relationships that wouldn't exist had I not started serving at my local church.

LOCAL NONPROFITS LIKE THRIFT STORES OR FOOD PANTRIES

This is a great activity no matter what, but especially great to do with teams or coworkers. Serving others feeds your soul, and sometimes you need to step out of the comfort of your day-to-day and do something for others. Selfless motives aside, it is a great way to meet new people. Whether it's the coordinators of the food pantry, or the others who decided to serve that day, you're going to meet some really interesting people.

My team and I once served at a local nonprofit

called BEAM in Jacksonville Beach, where they have a food pantry. We chose to work in the garden, and I met a man who is now retired and who would serve about every week. He spent the majority of his life in the corporate world as a high-level executive, and he and I have since gotten coffee periodically, and he's been able to give me some invaluable, much-needed leadership advice.

I would have never received such timely advice had I never met him by spending a day serving.

WALK AROUND YOUR NEIGHBORHOOD, THE BEACH, OR A LOCAL PARK AND CLEAN UP TRASH

We host a monthly group workout called Faith and Fitness in Jacksonville Beach, where I do a short devotional and lead a workout; then as a group, we take gloves and trash bags and walk the beach during the busy, messy parts of the year. As we walk the beach, we have met so many interesting people. The group itself has grown over the years simply because as we meet new people on the beach, we invite them to come the next month!

Not only is this a great way to create connections,

but it's a fantastic way to publicly inspire change in your community.

TIP #5: HANG OUT WITH YOUR FRIENDS, WHEN THEY'RE NOT HANGING OUT WITH YOUR FRIENDS.

You know what I'm talking about...

You know those times when a friend of yours invites you out, and you ask, "Who's going?" and they respond with a group of people you may not know, or at least not know that well? This is what I'm talking about. I usually avoid these situations because, honestly, I like my small circles. But when I recognize that I need to expand my network, then I take a step out of my comfort zone and say yes to these opportunities. Being open-minded about hanging out with different groups of people (as long as their values or activities aren't immoral or generally uncomfortable) can really expand your connection capacity.

Abraham Lincoln was well known for putting people in his cabinet who thought quite differently from him. While many would find this threatening, he realized he had blind spots in his own thinking and needed people who were strong in the areas that he was weak in. This helped him form a strong multi-faceted team that was seldom caught off guard because they had not thought of all aspects of an issue.

There are plenty of benefits of creating connections outside of your normal circle, but here are three main ones:

BENEFIT #1: GAIN A DIFFERENT PERSPECTIVE ON EVERYTHING.

When you hang out with the same people all of the time, you will most likely all begin to share a lot of the same views toward everything from politics to your favorite color. By spending time with diverse groups—whether it's different race, nationality, beliefs, or even hobbies—you will see into the minds of people who think and live completely different than you. This will allow you to have an increased self-awareness, empathy, and acceptance of others.

BENEFIT #2: BE MORE CREATIVE.

Your friends are most often going to have a bias toward your creativity. Most of the time, groups of people dress somewhat the same, talk the same, and like the same things. But creativity is rarely birthed from doing the "same." The creator of Red Bull got his idea on a work trip to a completely different country, so your next great idea could be by hanging out with some new people.

BENEFIT #3: MAKE BETTER DECISIONS.

Having people around us who are able to see situations from many different angles helps us to get a more complete and clearer picture from which we can make more-informed decisions.

Also, your friends already know you so well, and you know them well. When we spend a lot of time with people, we grow to assume that they know what we know, so we may contribute less to decision making over time because we "already know what they'll say." As odd as it sounds, people sometimes value strangers' opinions more, which could ultimately contribute to your decisions about things.

A mentor of mine used to say, "You are just one connection away from a breakthrough," so I hope by now, you can understand the value in that statement. Making connections is fun and exciting once you begin to commit to the consistency required to do so, and I can't wait for you to start seeing the benefits.

As we transition into this next chapter, make sure to reflect on the answers to those questions when we started. This next chapter might be my favorite, because it's almost entirely measurable and, in most instances, costs you nothing but a little time.

CHAPTER 4

COMPETENCE

"Trust is a function of both character and competence. Of course, you can't trust someone who lacks integrity, but if someone is honest but they can't perform, you're not going to trust them either."

—STEPHEN COVEY

Personally, I love this area of growth because it is the most quantifiable. What you know can be measured and, therefore, can be acted upon. People always say, "Knowledge is power," but that's only a part of it. It's what we do with our knowledge that counts, and if you are struggling to reach your goals in life, this is a great place to start.

A few more questions before we get started:

1. When was the last time you learned, read, or studied something, without having to do it for homework or for work?

2. Has your lack of knowledge in an area ever held you back from reaching a goal?

3. Are you the type to act on new information, or just store it?

HOW DO WE GROW OUR COMPETENCE LEVEL?
TIP #1: LISTEN MORE, TALK LESS.

Ralph Waldo Emerson said, "Every man is my superior, in that, I learn of him." Which basically means that we can learn something from everyone. Unfortunately, most of us would rather talk than listen. You'd be amazed by how much people have to offer if you take the time to pay attention to what they are saying rather than be consumed with the thoughts about what you are going to say in response. In the book *The 7 Habits of Highly Effective People*, Steven Covey outlines in his fifth habit, which is "Seek First to Understand, Then to Be Understood," the importance of transitioning from watching people talk while we think about what we're going to say

to what he calls "active and empathetic listening."
I have defined these types of listening below:

- **Active listening** is a technique that is used in counseling, training, and solving disputes or conflicts. It requires that the listener fully concentrate, understand, respond, and then remember what is being said and sometimes involves repeating back what has been said.[20]

- **Empathetic listening** is paying attention to another person with emotional identification, compassion, feeling, and insight. One basic principle is to connect emotionally with another person while simultaneously attempting to connect cognitively.[21]

It takes a lot of concentration and determination to be a better listener. Becoming an active and empathetic listener is about developing completely new habits, which means you'll have to get rid of old habits, and old habits are hard to break. If your listening skills are anywhere near as bad as mine, then you'll need to do a lot of work over time to make this change.

THERE ARE SEVEN KEY TECHNIQUES YOU CAN USE TO DEVELOP YOUR ACTIVE LISTENING SKILLS.

TECHNIQUE #1: APPROACH EACH CONVERSATION WITH A GOAL TO LEARN SOMETHING.

Before you engage in a conversation, make the conscious decision that you are going to intentionally learn something. If you're type A (like me), goal setting is a huge hack when it comes to interpersonal exchanges. I try to set a goal of remembering people's names, and because of that, I am much better at remembering names than I used to be. If you apply this to your conversations, you will become a much better listener right away.

TECHNIQUE #2: PAY ATTENTION.

This involves eliminating distractions.

Put your phone away or turn it upside down. I have to do this because I have a really hard time focusing. If a text pops up on my phone, either I'm going to look down and check it, or I have to consciously avoid looking down. Both take my attention away from who is talking. The same goes for any other type of distractions, such as email, a project you might be working on, or whatever show you've got on, or even music in the background.

TECHNIQUE #3: SHOW THAT YOU'RE LISTENING.

Don't look down or around while the other person is talking. Make a comfortable (but not creepy) amount of eye contact, and nod when necessary to acknowledge that you're following along. Encourage the person you're talking to to keep talking by giving short affirmations like, "Yes," "Okay," and, "Uh-huh."

TECHNIQUE #4: ASK QUESTIONS.

You can't expect everyone to be great communicators. A lot of people have a hard time making their point or telling a good story. Asking them questions helps them along the process at the same time it gives you a greater understanding and more clarity, and it shows that you're listening.

There are two types of questions to ask in a conversation:

1. **Clarification**—This is when you literally don't understand something that they said, so you are asking in order to gain clarity. This isn't rhetorical or short-sided (and sometimes you need to let them know that).

   Example: "Wait a second. A second ago, you said XYZ. I didn't really understand what you meant. Can you explain that to me?"

2. **Confirmation**—This helps move on to another topic or part of a story and lets the speaker know that you are tracking along. Additionally, it might create more value in the conversation by creating emphasis.

   Example: "No way! So, she really XYZ'd?"

TECHNIQUE #5: PROVIDE FEEDBACK
WHEN THE TIME IS RIGHT.

There will come a time when the person you're speaking to allows for a response, or for some type of feedback. They most likely won't say, "What's your feedback?" He or she might just pause for a second after telling you something with the expectation of you responding. This is your opportunity to tell them what you think. Do your best to give a nonbiased response, especially if you don't know this person very well. If this is someone you do know well, judgment and some form of bias might be inevitable, so always make sure to give context.

Example: "You know I love you, but since we were kids, you always do XYZ."

TECHNIQUE #6: EMBRACE AWKWARD SILENCES.

Unlike the above instance, this is usually an obvious moment of necessary silence. Maybe the speaker is getting emotional, or just trying to gather their thoughts. Most of us are so conditioned to expecting others to butt in during a pause, so the speaker might be rushing to get their point across and fumbling over their thoughts. This is your opportunity to show the speaker that you are present, and you are paying attention, and what they are saying matters.

TECHNIQUE #7: RESPOND APPROPRIATELY.

Now that you've listened intently, you've asked the

right questions, and you've allowed the speaker to get everything out, you should have a level-headed, educated, and relevant response. Whether this is a conversation or an argument, now is your time to respond. Be candid and honest, but assert yourself respectfully.

Start using these techniques today to become a better listener, communicator, friend, spouse, coworker, and leader.

TIP #2: READ MORE.

Here are some of my favorite quotes about reading:

"A reader lives a thousand lives before he dies...The man who never reads lives only one."

—GEORGE R. R. MARTIN

"The reading of all good books is like conversation with the finest (people) of the past centuries."

—DESCARTES

"The more that you read, the more things you will know. The more that you learn, the more places you'll go."

—DR. SEUSS

"Books are a uniquely portable magic."

—STEPHEN KING

"There is more treasure in books than in all the pirate's loot on Treasure Island."

—WALT DISNEY

"One glance at a book and you hear the voice of another person, perhaps someone dead for one thousand years. To read is to voyage through time."

—CARL SAGAN

"If we encounter a man of rare intellect, we should ask him what books he reads."

—RALPH WALDO EMERSON

"Books serve to show a man that those original thoughts of his aren't very new after all."

—ABRAHAM LINCOLN

"Show me a family of readers, and I will show you the people who move the world."

—NAPOLEON BONAPARTE

"To acquire the habit of reading is to construct for yourself a refuge from almost all the miseries of life."

—W. SOMERSET MAUGHAM

"If you don't like to read, you haven't found the right book."

—J. K. ROWLING

"Employ your time in improving yourself by other men's writings so that you shall come easily by what others have labored hard for."

—SOCRATES

It's been said time and time again that "leaders are readers." I always tell our staff or anyone I mentor that everything good I know or any wisdom I have, I either learned the hard way, or I read it somewhere. And trust me, you don't want to learn the lessons that I've learned the hard way. Reading is a wayyy safer route! In short, reading is our way of learning things the easy way, getting to know people, or exploring the world without ever leaving our seat. Aside from that, here are some additional benefits of reading regularly:

IMPROVED EMPATHY AND EQ

Research has shown that people who read literary fiction—stories that explore the inner lives of characters—show a heightened ability to understand the feelings and beliefs of others.

Researchers call what we would call empathy the "theory of mind," a set of skills essential for building, navigating, and maintaining social relationships.

While a single session of reading literary fiction isn't likely to spark this feeling, the research shows that long-term fiction readers do tend to have a better-developed sense of empathy toward others.[22]

IMPROVED CREATIVITY

The more we read, the more enlightened we become. Gaining knowledge empowers our minds and broadens its range.

Reading broadens our imagination by stimulating the right side of our brain. It literally opens our minds to new possibilities and new ideas, helping us experience and analyze the world through others' lives.

Neuroscientists at Emory University discovered that reading fiction can improve brain function on a variety of levels. They found that becoming engrossed in a novel enhances connectivity in the brain and improves brain function. Reading fiction was found to improve the reader's imagination in a way that is similar to muscle memory in sports.[23]

IMPROVED FOCUS AND CONCENTRATION

Reading not only improves your brain's connectivity, but it also increases attention spans, focus, and concentration.

If you struggle to focus, reading can improve your attention span.

When you read a book, all of your attention is focused on the story or in gaining a better understanding of a particular topic—the rest of the world just falls away, and you can immerse yourself in every fine detail you're absorbing.

Books with better structures encourage us to think in sequence—the more we read, the more our brains are able to link cause and effect.[24]

IMPROVED VOCABULARY AND COMMUNICATION SKILLS

Reading researchers as far back as the 1960s have discussed what's known as "the Matthew effect," a term that refers to biblical verse Matthew 13:12: "Whoever has will be given more, and they will have an abundance. Whoever does not have, even what they have will be taken from them."

The Matthew effect sums up the idea that the rich get richer and the poor get poorer—a concept that applies as much to vocabulary as it does to money.

Researchers have found that students who read books regularly, beginning at a young age, gradually develop large vocabularies.[25] And vocabulary size can influence many areas of your life, from scores on standardized tests to college admissions and job opportunities.

A 2019 poll conducted by Cengage showed that 69 percent of employers are looking to hire people with "soft" skills, like the ability to communicate effectively.[26] Reading books is the best way to increase your exposure to new words, learned in context.

IMPROVED IQ

People who exhibit strong reading skills early in life grow up to be more intelligent. That was the finding of a study published in 2014 that measured the cognitive development of 1,890 sets of identical twins. When two twins shared the same genes and home environments, early reading skills appeared to be the factor that decided which twin would be better at both verbal tests (like vocabulary) and nonverbal tests (like reasoning tests). Because reading ability is something that's learned, the study authors concluded that more emphasis should be placed on teaching strong reading skills to young children.[27]

DECREASED LEVELS OF STRESS

In 2009, a group of researchers measured the effects of yoga, humor, and reading on the stress levels of students in demanding health science programs in the United States.

The study found that thirty minutes of reading lowered blood pressure, heart rate, and feelings of psychological distress just as effectively as yoga and humor did.

The authors concluded, "Since time constraints are one of the most frequently cited reasons for high stress levels reported by health science students, thirty minutes of one of these techniques can be easily incorporated into their schedule without diverting a large amount of time from their studies."[28]

IMPROVED WRITING SKILLS

A well-read writer has a better vocabulary, recognizes the nuances of language, and distinguishes between poor and quality writing.

Author and writing teacher Roz Morris has a great take on this. "Reading exposes us to other styles, other voices, other forms, and other genres of writing. Importantly, it exposes us to writing that's better than our own and helps us to improve. Reading—the good and the bad—inspires you."

Another writer you may have heard of, Stephen King, said: "Can I be blunt on this subject? If you don't have time to read, you don't have the time (or the tools) to write. Simple as that."

Reading helps us make connections to our own experiences and emotions, so reading makes you a better writer and a better communicator.[29]

TIP #3: BE MORE THOROUGH WITH EXISTING PROJECTS.

Let me explain. As professionals, students, parents, etc., we are always going to be working on some type of "project." In my experience, people can often rush through projects for one of two reasons: either you have done this plenty of times and have grown comfortable, or it's something new that you aren't very interested in. Whatever the case, often by slowing down, whether it's something we want to do or not, we can learn and grow a lot more by being thorough and attentive. Only you will know what this really means for you.

TIP #4: LEARN TO ASK BETTER QUESTIONS.

First of all, the benefits of asking questions far outweigh the cost. So, if you aren't a question-asker, I suggest becoming one. Asking questions is linked to higher intelligence and higher likability, especially when you're doing it right.

When I was a kid, I would ask wayyyy too many questions. I'm sure most kids did, but I was so bad that, eventually, my dad restricted me to ten questions a day—and he was serious. Because of that, it taught me how to ask good questions. If I didn't, he'd stop talking to me by noon on the weekends!

How do we ask better questions? Before asking anyone else, ask yourself these questions:

- "Do I already know the answer to this?"

- "Can I easily find the answer to this on Google?"

- "Can I find the answer to this in a previous email, text message, or any existing material around me?"

If the answer is "no" to all of those, then it's time to construct a well-outlined, concise question. Don't be short, and don't be vague. But also, don't be too elaborate or abstract. People who get asked questions want to genuinely answer them, but if that is too much of a challenge, then both of you will feel like a failure.

Once you master the art of asking the right questions, there are a ton of benefits!

- Better working and social relationships

- Creating clarity around topics you or others may not have understood

- Consistent organizational or relational progress

- Encouraging breakthrough thinking with your team

- Empowering others to learn more alongside you

TIP #5: TAKE AN ONLINE COURSE.

This is one of the more practical solutions to stretching your competency level, and there are so many avenues you can go in. The benefits of continued education are clear, but most people just don't know how easy it is to find affordable and convenient avenues to continue learning after high school or college. Below are a few free or affordable options where you can learn from schools such as

Duke, Harvard, MIT, and Stanford—or you can learn specific skills and trades:

UDEMY

Udemy is an American online learning platform aimed at professional adults and students. As of January 2020, the platform has more than fifty million students and 57,000 instructors teaching courses in over sixty-five languages. There have been over 295 million course enrollments.

COURSERA

Coursera is a worldwide online learning platform founded in 2012 by Stanford computer science professors Andrew Ng and Daphne Koller that offers massive open online courses, specializations, and degrees.

EDX

edX is a massive open online course provider. It hosts online university-level courses in a wide range of disciplines to a worldwide student body, including some courses at no charge. It also conducts research into learning based on how people use its platform.

SKILLSHARE

Skillshare is an American online learning community for people who want to learn from educational videos. The courses, which are not accredited, are available through subscription. The majority of courses focus on interaction rather than lecturing, with the primary goal of learning by completing a project.

By the time you are reading this, chances are there are multiple other online learning platforms. Considering everything that has (or had) happened in 2020, they might even offer credits toward a degree.

We have to remember that knowledge without action is worthless. Make sure, as you continue learning and growing, that you not only apply what you learn, but you do your best to teach others along the way.

That leads us into our next and possibly most uncomfortable chapter so far.

CHAPTER 5

CHARACTER

"Most people say that it's the intellect which makes a great scientist. They are wrong: it is character."

—ALBERT EINSTEIN

"How true Daddy's words were when he said: all children must look after their own upbringing. Parents can only give good advice or put them on the right paths, but the final forming of a person's character lies in their own hands."

—ANNE FRANK

"Knowledge will give you power, but character respect."

—BRUCE LEE

"You can easily judge the character of a man by how he treats those who can do nothing for him."

—JAMES D. MILES

"The measure of a man's real character is what he would do if he knew he would never be found out."

—THOMAS B. MACAULAY

This one is so important that it deserved multiple quotes. I'm really trying to drive this one home, and I needed some help by the greats like Albert, Bruce and Anne. I figure...if you won't listen to me, maybe you'll listen to them.

Honestly, this might be the most important one. You can be the smartest, most confident person in the room, but if you have a desperately flawed character, those things won't get you very far.

We can all agree that this can be a touchy subject. If you've gotten to this section and feel uncomfortable, it is most likely a sign that you need to lean in the most here. Consider this book your private journal.

WHAT IS "CHARACTER" AND
WHY IS IT IMPORTANT?

Technically, "character" is a morally neutral term. Everyone, from the well-known saints like Mother Teresa, to the most despicable examples of evil like Adolph Hitler, have a character. The term is used to describe a person's most noticeable attributes; it's the compilation of all their features and traits that define them and their individual nature.

To say that a person has a "good character" (which is the goal here) doesn't require them to be perfect, but it does mean that we consider them worthy of our trust and admiration.

As in Anne Frank's quote, we know that people aren't inherently good or bad. No one is born with a virtuous character; it's something that is developed over time. In our early years, it's developed primarily by our surroundings and our upbringing. As we grow and mature, we are more and more responsible for the positive development of our character.

Character is also not defined by a single moment or action, but by your habits over time. It's defined by your consistent adherence to generally accepted moral values, not by the things you say or "intend" to do. Virtues transcend cultural, religious, and socioeconomic differences—like trustworthiness, respect, responsibility, fairness, caring, and citizenship.

People of good character are guided by ethical principles even when it's physically dangerous or detrimental to their careers, social standing, or economic well-being. They do the right thing even when it costs more than they can afford to pay.[30]

So from what we've learned, character is both formed and revealed by how we deal with everyday situations as well as extraordinary pressures and temptations. Like a well-made tower, character is built stone by stone, decision by decision.

The way we treat people we think can't help or hurt us—like strangers, waiters, and subordinates—tells more about our character than how we treat people we think are important. How we behave when we think no one is looking or when we don't think we will get caught more accurately portrays our character than what we say or do in service of our reputations.

SO, HOW DO WE STRENGTHEN
OUR CHARACTER?

I think the first step is acknowledging that all of us, no matter how "good" we think we are, can grow in character. Some of us much more than others.

Asking yourself these questions below, and making some notes, would be a great step two:

1. On a scale of one to ten, with ten being "extremely generous" and one being "extremely selfish," where would you rate yourself?

2. On a scale of one to ten, with ten being "extremely supportive" and one being "extremely critical" of others, where would you rate yourself?

3. How comfortable are you with being wrong?

4. How often do you lie? When you do, how do you feel?

5. How often do you compliment others? When you do, is it organic, or do you have an agenda?

6. Would you say you treat strangers, waiters, and

subordinates as well as the people you look up to?

7. When bad things happen in your life, do you take personal responsibility or do you most often see yourself as a victim?

8. How often do you let your emotions like anger or bitterness affect your relationships with others?

9. Are you the same person on social media that you are behind closed doors?

10. Do the people closest to you know the real you?

After you spend some time thinking through your notes, here are the practical tips to grow in character:

TIP #1: PRACTICE MORE HONESTY AND INTEGRITY.

This isn't to say that you aren't already an honest person with some level of integrity, but I think everyone can grow in this area. Some people think of honesty as simply not lying, but it's more than that. Honesty and integrity are also:

- Being more sincere in your feedback

- Telling people how you feel

- Doing what you say you will do and communicating or apologizing when you can't.

- Recognizing that "white lies" are still lies

TIP #2: LEARN EMPATHY.

"Empathy" means the ability to understand and share the feelings and experiences of another. In other words, empathy is imagining yourself in someone else's skin: feeling what they feel and seeing yourself and the world from their point of view.[31] Empathy is one of the most important character traits you can acquire in your lifetime, but it is also the hardest—since it is virtually impossible to put ourselves in other people's shoes without actually experiencing what they have. Here are a few ways to grow in empathy:

- Become a better listener.

- Serve at a local homeless outreach or do a mission trip.

- Spend time alone thinking, praying, or meditating about and for others.

- When dealing with someone in certain challenging scenarios, ask yourself these two questions:

  ◦ "If I were them, would I want to be treated this way?"

  ◦ "How would I realistically act in this scenario if I were them?"

TIP #3: EXPRESS GRATITUDE.

If a tree falls in a forest and no one is around to hear it, does it make a sound? Who knows...but that's what I think of when I think about people who don't express gratitude. Being grateful for others is great, but if no one knows, what real good does it do? I believe that gratitude is more than a feeling, and it should most often be expressed as a verb. Tell others that you are thankful for them, show them with your actions, and do it consistently. Since I am a creature of habit and am easily distracted, this is actually something I have in my daily to-do list. I try to make a point every day to let someone know in my life—whether it's from a text, a call, buying a coffee, setting a dinner date, etc.—that I love them and am thankful for them. And if it's a stranger, like the barista or the guy who just changed your tires, always make sure to express an honest level of gratitude.

TIP #4: BECOME MORE SELF-AWARE.

Most people think that they know themselves pretty well but have never really spent the time alone to view themselves from a third-person point of view or tried to understand why they do the things they do. Self-awareness is a key component to emotional intelligence and growing in your character. Understanding this allows you to better understand your personal strengths, weaknesses, values, and habits. Here are a few ways to increase in self-awareness:

1. Begin to look at yourself more objectively by journaling regularly.

2. Take personality tests.

3. Begin practicing meditation or prayer.

4. Establish daily, weekly, monthly, and yearly goals.

TIP #5: ASK FOR FEEDBACK.

We will never really know what people think of us unless we ask. We have to listen to the feedback of our friends, family, and coworkers so we can let them play a role in helping us grow. Tell your friends when you are looking for open, honest, critical, and objective perspectives. Allow your friends to feel safe while they are giving you an informal yet honest view. Keep in mind, this process requires humility. Here are two simple questions I recommend asking those who know you pretty well:

1. "What are my blind spots or weaknesses?"

2. "What are some things I'm really good at?"

Whew! If you made it through that without giving up or sending me a nasty DM, I'm proud of you. It takes a lot of humility to recognize that, no matter who you are, you can always work on growing in character.

Everything we've covered so far can be accomplished fairly well with quantifiable action and some sort of to-do list, but this next one is a little more abstract—and possibly the most challenging for me to consistently commit to growing in.

CHAPTER 6

CLARITY

"More important than the quest for certainty is the quest for clarity."

—FRANCOIS GAUTIER

I just feel like, at least in my life, things can all get jumbled up together in my mind so that it feels like I am walking around with one of those balls full of rubber bands in my brain. Whether it's projects, work stuff, hobbies, plans, responsibilities, etc., they all seem to get mixed in with each other and begin to decrease my effectiveness, which is counterintuitive to a life of consistent growth.

That's when I know that I need to take a step back, audit my current lifestyle, and then apply one of the following steps.

Before we continue, let's find out if you need more clarity in your life by asking some questions:

1. Have you ever been described as "running around like a chicken with your head cut off," or at least felt that way? Are you always like that, or just in certain seasons of life? Why do you think that is?

2. When was the last time you spent an entire twenty-four hours by yourself?

3. How much time a day do you spend in front of a screen?

4. On a scale of one to ten, how do you think your friends and coworkers would rate your strength in communication?

HOW DO WE GAIN MORE CLARITY?

We live in what's being called the Digital Transformation Era. With almost everything available at the touch of our fingers, and so much stimulation all around us, it is easy to get and stay distracted. Most of us are distracted in our lives right now but have grown so comfortable with this new normal that we don't even realize it. One of the best ways to stretch yourself is by intentionally gaining clarity, and here are a few ways.

TIP #1: CONSISTENTLY COMMUNICATE.

According to a survey by the National Association of Colleges and Employers, communication skills are listed as the most important quality sought in job candidates.[32] Oftentimes, our capacity is limited by our inability to communicate properly. Although we live in the Digital Transformation Era, consistent (and quality) communication is more important than ever. Communication is not a one-way street, though. It includes both giving and receiving well. By asking the right questions and learning to actively listen and effectively communicate your thoughts, ideas, and emotions, you can clear up a lot of distractions and become much more productive. I talked about "asking the right questions" in chapter 4 and "being more honest" in chapter 5, so make sure to revisit those if you need.

Some of the most famous leaders in our history became known as such primarily through their ability to communicate. People like Winston Churchill, Billy Graham, Abraham Lincoln...the list goes on.

Unfortunately, in school we are taught all sorts of subjects, from math to writing to science, but no curriculum or practical teaching is developed around the importance of communication. Whether you're a leader, pastor, manager, advertiser, salesperson, or even just a spouse, the inability to communicate well will cripple your potential.

HERE ARE A FEW EXAMPLES OF WHERE COMMUNICATION CAN MAKE OR BREAK YOU.

- You are an entry-level employee, who has outperformed expectations, and you want to properly and professionally request a raise.

- You're an up-and-coming youth pastor who is asked to teach a few Sundays to the entire congregation, and this will be your first time teaching to a general audience, as opposed to a group of young people.

- You're a marketing specialist, who has most often performed the work that was asked of you, and now you'd like to convey a great idea you had for the next series of ads.

- You have built a business plan, and you want to pitch it to an investor or group of investors or to the bank for a loan.

- You've been dating this new girl for a short period of time, and there's something you'd like to address about the relationship that makes you uncomfortable.

The examples are literally endless.

SO HOW DO WE GET BETTER WITH COMMUNICATION?

Here are the ten methods to improve your communication skills:

1. Recognize the importance of communication and commit to being better. Take classes, read books, listen to podcasts, watch TED Talks, watch YouTube videos, read magazine articles, or learn from successful communicators around you.

2. Be short and sweet. **Use simple, straightfor-
    ward, and understandable language for the
    audience or the person you're speaking to.**
    Don't try to explain calculus to a third-grader.
    Remember that Lincoln's Gettysburg Address
    was 286 words, about two minutes long.

3. Engage your audience. Be humble enough to
    ask for help, and let your spouse, friends, and/
    or coworkers know that you are working on your
    communications skills, and give them permis-
    sion to give you feedback.

4. Take time to respond. After you've listened (and
    understood), take time to "draft" in your head
    what you want to say.

5. **Add "novelty" to improve memory reten-
    tion with the audience.** A study[33] showed that
    people generally retain more information when
    presented with novel, as opposed to routine,
    situations. To help audience members retain
    information, consider using some sort of novel
    event in a presentation or whatever message
    you are trying to get out. This might be some-

thing funny, or something that simply catches people by surprise.

6. Make sure you are understood. Don't just assume that since you followed the steps, everyone will automatically understand. Instead, look for ways to clarify or rephrase what you are trying to say so it can be understood. I often ask the question, "Does that make sense?" and I make sure whomever I am speaking to is comfortable asking questions (unless it's a large audience).

7. Be a good listener. The best communicators are almost always the best listeners. Listen without judgment, and don't be distracted by thinking about what you want to say next or by your phone or whatever is next on your agenda. Then, respond, don't react.

8. Pay attention to body language. Studies show that nonverbal communication accounted for 55 percent of how an audience perceived a presenter. That means that the majority of what you say is communicated not through words

but through physical cues.[34] To communicate clearly and confidently, adopt proper posture. Avoid slouching, folding your arms, or making yourself appear smaller than you are. Instead, fill up the space you are given, maintain eye contact, and (if appropriate) move around the space, but don't move around too much! Also, watch for visual signs that your listener understands, agrees, or disagrees with your message.

9. Establish and maintain eye contact. Whether speaking to a crowd or to one person, maintaining eye contact builds credibility and demonstrates you care about your listeners. Just don't be weird about it.

10. Make your audience a priority. As I said earlier, communication is a two-way street. Even if you're the one with an agenda, for your message to be accepted, you have to prioritize whomever it is you are speaking to. You should sincerely care about the needs and the unique perspectives of those to whom you are communicating. One of the best ways to show your respect is simply by paying attention to what they say and

practicing empathy prior to and during the presentation or conversation.

TIP #2: FAST.

If you practice organized religion, you'll be familiar with this concept in a slightly different context. But for the same reasons why religious people fast in order to gain clarity and become closer to their creator, fasting from distractions can help you clear your mind and gain more control of your thoughts in order to grow. Whatever distracts you might be different than what distracts the next person, but it could be anything from social media to Netflix to binge eating. For example, try to take a day or two a week off of social media or television, and see how much more productive and clear your days can be.

TIP #3: ELIMINATE (OR CREATE A TO-DON'T LIST).

Over time, we accumulate roles, responsibilities, and habits that we simply don't need to be doing anymore. Also, it's possible that there are hobbies, habits, and friendships that may not be conducive to the future you've envisioned for yourself. At the end of each month or beginning of each new month, take one to two hours to sit, reflect, and document the things that have added up in your day-to-day. Once you've established a few, add them to your to-don't list. For those things that are holding you back from becoming the leader you were born to be, they need to be eliminated, and only you know what or who they are.

TIP #4: EAT BETTER.

Yes, I'm a fitness guy, so of course I'm going to bring up eating healthy, but there's more to it than that. Countless studies have shown how eating excess amounts of processed foods, saturated fats, and simple sugars can negatively affect our cognition and ability to focus. By eating a diet rich in whole foods, vitamins, and minerals, you are empowering your brain and body to grow and, in turn, become smarter and stronger. Oftentimes, our grogginess could have much more to do with our diet than needing another coffee. Here are a few basic tips to begin your healthier eating journey:

1. Remember balance is key. Try the 70/30 principle.

2. Track your calories with apps like MyFitness Pal.

3. Commit to eating fast food less.

4. Try a meal-prep company.

5. Get an accountability partner to join you.

TIP #5: LEARN TO SAY NO.

"I'm actually as proud of the things we haven't done as the things I have done. Innovation is saying no to one thousand things."

—STEVE JOBS

"The difference between successful people and very successful people is that very successful people say 'no' to almost everything."

—WARREN BUFFETT

Like I mentioned in the beginning of this chapter, my brain can feel like one of those rubber-band balls, all jumbled up and tightly wound—and it's usually because I've made too many commitments or put too much on my plate.

Some of us waste too much time and energy doing things we don't enjoy or things that don't add value simply because we don't know how to politely decline our friends, family, and coworkers when they invite us to things or ask us to do things. In turn, it becomes difficult to maintain a relative level of clarity in life. Your vision for your future gets skewed, and you become too "busy" to really make any progress. Please take this into context and know that I am not advising you to tell your spouse or your boss no, because some things need to be done and aren't negotiable, but common sense will give you an idea of the things in your life I'm referencing.

HERE ARE A FEW TIPS FOR SAYING NO.

- Ask if you can confirm later.

  For example, I get asked on the spot to do all kinds of things. Just like you, I'm sure. But I hate being unreliable, so I always check my calendar and my to-do list before I confirm anything.

  If I get asked to do something I most likely don't want to do, but I don't have the courage in the moment to say no (or maybe it would be impolite or too awkward), I will say something like, "I can most likely do that! When I get to the office in the morning, I will check my calendar for that day, then confirm whether I can or not!"

This gives me time to think about everything I have going on, and to also consider whether I really want to do this thing. I've gotten so used to saying no that maybe after thinking it through, it is actually something I want to do. Asking to confirm later allows me to not miss out on that opportunity, or to just politely decline later.

- Be honest.

  This is totally contextual, but most of the time, you can just be honest. If a coworker asks you to grab a drink after work, simply say, "No, thanks!"

  Be assertive in your response; being honest in your no will gain you a reputation for being a straightforward person, and most people really respect that.

- Explain why (if necessary), but don't make excuses.

This is similar to being honest, but more elaborate. If a friend asks if you want to go see a movie tomorrow night, don't make something up and say you have plans. Just politely say, "I would, but I'm trying to save money and I really need to catch up on some rest."

In these instances, I usually elaborate because I don't want to miss out on a future invite. In the above example with a coworker, that is typically when I have no interest in grabbing a drink with that person. But the times that I elaborate are the times when I am truly interested, but I just think I should allocate my time elsewhere.

- Keep it simple.

Once you've said "no," or briefly explained why you can't or don't want to, then leave it at that.

- Be confident and don't over-apologize.

Never feel obligated to others' time (unless it's

a spouse or superior when at work, duh). You have the right to prioritize yourself, and if you are overly apologetic about saying no, it will either seem ingenuine or that it's possible you can be convinced otherwise.

Learning to say no is a skill that takes time and effort to master, but it will help you gain and maintain clarity more than almost any other tip I can give you, not to mention all the other productivity benefits it will bring you.

TIP #6: GET ALONE.

This one is unusually hard for a lot of people. Humans crave community. Even introverts like to hang out with introverts. But sometimes we are compensating for our discomfort with loneliness by always surrounding ourselves with people. This is most people's unconscious way of never getting to know themselves, and never being able to sit with their thoughts. Whether it's taking a two-day trip by yourself to the woods, the mountains, the beach, or even a nearby staycation, or something as simple as going on a long walk with no music, getting alone consistently will stretch your ability to gain clarity in your life and grow as a leader.

I suggest making a habit out of it in small increments daily or weekly, so you rarely get to the point where you feel like you absolutely need to get away or just drop everything, because that isn't always a possible scenario depending on your work or family situation.

Greater clarity in life will strengthen your relationships with others and yourself, while allowing your brain the space to be proactive in its thinking, which leads to less stress and a higher quality of life. I hope by applying some of the above recommendations, you see the results and agree.

So 5 out of 6 Ways are done. Are you ready to live a life of never-ending growth? I hope so! But...all those Ways would be nothing without applying this next one, consistently, for the rest of your life.

Dun dun dunnn.

CHAPTER 7

COMMITMENT

"Inaction breeds doubt and fear. Action breeds confidence and courage. If you want to conquer fear, do not sit home and think about it. Go out and get busy."

—DALE CARNEGIE

We all know that one person, and it might even be you, who is always starting and stopping something. The things they start might even be great ideas! But they never see them through to completion. This type of habit might seem harmless, especially if the starting and stopping isn't directly affecting anyone else, but over time, it's a very detrimental character flaw.

If you want to accomplish anything great in life, you have to be committed.

A few more questions before we dive in:

1. How often do you start new things (projects, goals, etc.) and never see them through to completion?

2. Do people think of you as someone who always follows through on your commitments?

3. How much different would your life look like if you followed through on all the things that you set out to do?

4. What are your goals right now?

HOW DO I GET BETTER AT COMMITMENT?

As our world continues to evolve, everyone has more options. Unfortunately, this can lead to a lack of commitment, which results in you jumping from job to job, relationship to relationship, fitness trend to fitness trend, and diet to diet. You can't gain long-term results if you don't make long-term commitments, and this is one of the best ways to grow.

TIP #1: SET GOALS.

We covered this in the second chapter, but it's definitely worth revisiting at this point. Setting goals makes the ambitions in your head and the potential commitments you want to make real, especially if you write them down and begin to strategize how to accomplish them. This is how I would go about beginning to set goals: use the SMART method (covered in chapter 2).

TIP #2: TELL YOUR FRIENDS.

After you've set some SMART goals and written them down somewhere you will see them often, then you need to tell your friends and ask them to hold you accountable. Having the right accountability will inevitably increase your ability to commit—especially to things that are hard. Make sure you tell the right people, though!

Here are a few dos and don'ts of what I mean:

- DO tell your fitness-junkie friend about your new exercise goal.

- DON'T tell your friends who never go to the

gym and don't prioritize fitness to hold you accountable to your new fitness goals. It still might be good to tell them about your new goal in order to inspire them, but don't expect them to hold you accountable.

- DO tell your finance friend about your plan to save money.

- DON'T tell your buddy who is bad with money, and always trying to get you to do things, to hold you accountable to saving money. It still might be good to tell them about your new goal in order to inspire them, but don't expect them to hold you accountable.

- DO tell your coworkers that you want to start cursing less, or eating healthier at lunch, or walking on your break.

You get my drift...

TIP #3: TAKE ACTION.

Setting goals and telling your friends is a waste of time if you don't take action. And the last person you want to be known as is the person who was always hyped on their goals but never accomplished or even tried them. Eventually, your friends will stop taking you seriously. After you've set all your goals and created accountability, it's time to strategize and get to work.

Here are two examples:

- Goal #1: Read one book a month.

    ◦ Strategy: The average book is 150 pages long, which is five pages a day.

    ◦ Daily Action: Read five pages a day.

- Goal #2: Lose thirty pounds in six months.

    ◦ Strategy: There are twenty-six weeks in six months, so I need to lose 1.15 pounds per week. There are 3,500 calories in one pound, so I need to burn or create a caloric deficit of 4,025 calories per week.

    ◦ Daily Action: That is 575 calories a day. So if I burn 375 calories per day and eat 200 calories less per day, I will reach my goal.

TIP #4: WORK HARDER.

"Nobody cares. Work harder."

—CAMERON HANES

There is a principle I learned about while studying exercise science called the SAID principle. It's an acronym for "specific adaptations to imposed demands," which basically means that our bodies and our minds grow comfortable with our routines and can become stagnant or stop growing. If you do the same workout routine every day you go to the gym, your body will plateau. When you adapt to a certain weight, if your goal is to grow (or get stronger), you have to increase the weight, volume, or speed the next time you do that workout.

The same principle applies to any area of life. As you begin to set goals, strategize them, work toward them, and accomplish them, you will need to begin setting bigger, harder goals. If not, you will always stay the same, and that is counterintuitive to the idea of growth. Once you recognize that you've adapted to these new challenges, it's time to work harder.

How do we do this? Below I've outlined some ways to work harder and some practical examples:

- Surround yourself with people who motivate you to level up on a regular basis.

- Have easy-to-read reminders of your "why," and reference them regularly. Especially when you're having a hard time.

- Create positive reinforcements. For example, every time you finish a book, veg out on some Netflix for a few nights. If you get an A in your class, throw a party with some friends. If you have a successful week on your diet, eat a "cheat meal."

- Break up your larger projects/goals into smaller, more realistic ones. This makes them easier to wrap your head around.

PRACTICAL EXAMPLES

- Look at your goals last month or last year that you've accomplished, and set bigger ones.

- Read more books.

- Lift more weights.

- Run faster.

- Serve more people.

- Give more money or time.

Whatever it is for you, we can always work harder in order to grow our commitment muscle.

TIP #5: DON'T GIVE UP.

"It does not matter how slowly you go as long as you do not stop."

—CONFUCIUS

One part about goal setting that people rarely consider is that life is messy, and unexpected adversities present themselves all of the time. Very rarely do things work out as we plan them to, which can oftentimes be a good thing in the long run, but in order to find that out for yourself, you've got to see things through. In chapter 6, I talked about eliminating certain things in order to gain clarity, so don't take this piece of advice out of context. That was referring to habits and unproductive systems you have adopted over time. Also, sometimes in life, especially if certain things are toxic or destructive to our health, we need to let them go. For everything else, just don't give up.

There have been countless instances in my life where I was looking for a way out, and God blessed me with plenty of roadblocks so that I basically had no choice but to keep going.

In 2012, a few months after a large gym corporation bought out the smaller gym corporation that I was a manager for, I began looking for a way out. The quality of my work, the quality of my life, and my income had all been dramatically and negatively affected by this buyout, and I was questioning whether I should stay in the fitness industry altogether. Because I lived in Lakeland, Florida, and I had done sales my whole life, my solution was to transition to working at GEICO (they have a large headquarters in Lakeland). I figured I'd start out at about $45,000 a year and with my performance make some bonuses, get promoted, and live a life of comfort by making good money and working nine to five every day for a very successful company (which is a great gig if that's what your purpose is).

Although I knew that my place was in the fitness industry and leaving would mean giving up on my dreams, I was dead set on leaving. I was ready to give up. I went through the arduous interview process and got an offer. The last step was to do a hair follicle (drug) test. So, I went in, did the test, and awaited the results and my start date.

A few days later, even though I hadn't smoked weed in longer than I could remember, I was informed that I failed the drug test. It's possible it got in my hair from being around friends who smoke, but that's beside the point. I was devastated and, in a weird way, very relieved. Devastated because I had a girlfriend who made more money than me at the time, and her mom expected me to be the type of man with a steady income who could one day support a family. Relieved because although I had no idea what I would do next, besides continue working a job at a gym that I really disliked, I was hopeful that by staying on the path that God had called me to, it would work out.

It took a lot of hard work, a few big moves, and a few years, but all of that experience brought me to starting Superfit Foods, which is the company that I own and operate as I write this. Superfit Foods just celebrated five years, and despite the challenges of entrepreneurship, it has brought me the freedom and fulfillment I craved in the fitness industry all those years ago when I was ready to give up.

I consider myself lucky that my cowardly attempt to give up didn't work out, because it brought me to where I am now. But do yourself the favor of avoiding that altogether, and stay the course.

Commitment, even in the smallest form, every day over time, can make you a better friend, coworker, spouse, parent, leader, and entrepreneur. It will take commitment to accomplish all of the goals you've set in your life, including mastering the 6 Practical Ways to Never Stop Growing.

CONCLUSION

Let's recap...

Here are the six areas that, if you regularly reference them, can help you live a life of never-ending
growth:

1. CONFIDENCE

By changing our self-talk, taking better care of ourselves, setting goals, smiling more, and taking steps
of faith—our confidence will grow.

2. CONNECTIONS

By joining groups, leveraging social media, making
an effort to meet more people, and serving your
community—your connections will grow.

3. COMPETENCE

After learning to listen more, talk less, read more, and pursue continued education—both our EQ and our IG will grow.

4. CHARACTER

Regularly practicing integrity and honesty, learning empathy, expressing gratitude, becoming more self-aware and asking for feedback will dramatically increase the strength of your character.

5. CLARITY

Consistently communicating, fasting, eliminating, eating healthy, saying no, and being alone from time to time are going to be your keys to gaining and maintaining clarity in your life.

6. COMMITMENT

Setting goals, telling your friends, taking action, working hard, and never giving up are going to be the things that make you known as a reliable, committed leader.

I hope reading this book was as helpful for you as writing it was for me.

Much Love,

Jared Graybeal

ABOUT THE
AUTHOR

My mission is to encourage, educate, and empower others to live happier, healthier lives.

I'm a NASM Certified Personal Trainer, Fitness Nutrition Specialist, Behavioral Change Specialist, CrossFit Level 2 Trainer, and Corrective Exercise Specialist with an education in marketing and psychology from the University of North Florida.

I own and operate two companies. One is Superfit Foods, a healthy, subscription-based, fully customizable meal-prep company. The other is E3, a business consulting and marketing agency.

I've done a few cool things, like exhibiting Superfit Foods at Forbes Under 30 and giving a TEDx Talk on nutrition and mental health, and every day I get to work hard at doing what I love.

NOTES

1   "Just Three in 10 People Feel 'Happy with Their Lives,'" *The Telegraph*, published January 22, 2015, https://www.telegraph.co.uk/news/uknews/11362246/Just-three-in-10-people-feel-happy-with-their-lives.html.

2   "Nurse Reveals Top 5 Regrets of the Dying," Mindful, published July 27, 2016, https://www.mindful.org/no-regrets/.

3   "Success through Goal Setting, Part 1 of 3," Brian Tracy International, accessed October 15, 2020, https://www.briantracy.com/blog/personal-success/success-through-goal-setting-part-1-of-3/.

4   Nadja Walter, Lucie Nikoleizig, and Dorothy Alfermann, "Effects of Self-Talk Training on Competitive Anxiety, Self-Efficacy, Volitional Skills, and Performance: An Intervention Study with Junior Sub-Elite Athletes," *Sports* 7, no. 6 (2019): 148, https://doi.org/10.3390/sports7060148.

5   "Internal Monologue," Wikipedia, https://en.wikipedia.org/wiki/Internal_monologue.

6   Elizabeth Scott, "The Toxic Effects of Negative Self-Talk," Very Well Mind, last modified February 25, 2020, https://www.verywellmind.com/negative-self-talk-and-how-it-affects-us-4161304.

7   David Tod, James Hardy, and Emily Oliver, "Effects of Self-Talk: A Systematic Review," *Journal of Sport and Exercise Psychology* 33, no. 5 (2011): 666–87, https://doi.org/10.1123/jsep.33.5.666.

8   James L. Creighton, "Change Your Self-Talk: Examine Your Self-Talk to Be Sure It Is Serving You Well," *Psychology Today*, published November 5, 2019, https://www.psychologytoday.com/us/blog/loving-through-your-differences/201911/change-your-self-talk.

9   "Do's and Don'ts of Disciplining Dogs," Hill's, published May 8, 2018, https://www.hillspet.com/dog-care/routine-care/how-to-discipline-dog.

10 Fiona Macrae, "Smile! Why White Teeth Are a Sign of Good Health and Make You More Attractive," *DailyMail*, published August 1, 2012, https://www.dailymail.co.uk/news/article-2182380/Smile-Why-white-teeth-sign-good-health-make-attractive.html.

11 Stephanie Booth, "How to Stop Bad Bacteria in Your Mouth from Migrating to Your Brain," Healthline, published May 5, 2019, https://www.healthline.com/health-news/bacteria-in-your-mouth-can-find-its-way-to-your-brain.

12 Micah Abraham, "Anxiety and the Connection to Body Odor," CalmClinic, last modified October 10, 2020, https://www.calmclinic.com/anxiety/signs/body-odor.

13 Eric Suni, "Sleep Hygiene," Sleep Foundation, last modified August 14, 2020, https://www.sleepfoundation.org/articles/sleep-hygiene.

14 B. Rose Kelly, "In a Split Second, Clothes Make the Man More Competent in the Eyes of Others," Princeton School of Public and International Affairs, Princeton University, published December 9, 2019, https://spia.princeton.edu/news/split-second-clothes-make-man-more-competent-eyes-others.

15 "SMART Goals: How to Make Your Goals Achievable," MindTools, accessed October 15, 2020, https://www.mindtools.com/pages/article/smart-goals.htm.

16 "Law of Large Numbers," Wikipedia, https://en.wikipedia.org/wiki/Law_of_large_numbers.

17 "How A Smile Can Affect Self-Esteem: Building Healthy Relationships With A Positive Attitude," Brian Tracy International, accessed October 15, 2020, https://www.briantracy.com/blog/general/how-a-smile-can-affect-self-esteem-building-healthy-relationships-with-a-positive-attitude/.

18 "BNI (Organization), Wikipedia, https://en.wikipedia.org/wiki/
    BNI_(organization).

19 "Rotary International," Wikipedia, https://en.wikipedia.org/wiki/
    Rotary_International.

20 "Active Listening," Wikipedia, https://en.wikipedia.org/wiki/
    Active_listening.

21 W. Huitt, "Empathetic Listening," Educational Psychology Interactive,
    Valdosta State University, accessed October 15, 2020, http://www.
    edpsycinteractive.org/topics/process/listen.html.

22 Rebecca Joy, "Benefits of Reading Books: How It Can Positively Affect
    Your Life," Healthline, published October 15, 2019, https://www.
    healthline.com/health/benefits-of-reading-books#increases-empathy.

23 Paul Heavenridge, "Why Read? Reason #6: Knowledge is Power
    but Imagination is More Valuable," Literacy Works, published
    May 20, 2015, https://www.literacyworks.org/news/2015/5/20/
    why-read-reason-6-knowledge-is-power-but-imagination-is-more-
    valuable#:~:text=Reading%20broadens%20our%20imagination%20
    by,the%20world%20through%20others'%20lives.&text=They%20
    found%20that%20becoming%20engrossed,brain%20and%20
    improves%20brain%20function.

24 Thomas Oppong, "The Reading Brain (Why Your Brain Needs You
    to Read Every Day)," (blog), published February 20. 2018, https://
    thomas-oppong.medium.com/the-reading-brain-why-your-brain-
    needs-you-to-read-every-day-f5307c50d979#:~:text=Reading%20
    not%20only%20improves%20your,can%20improve%20your%20a-
    ttention%20span.&text=Books%20with%20better%20structures%20
    encourage,to%20link%20cause%20and%20effect.

25 Kate Cain and Jane Oakhill, "Matthew Effects in Young Readers:
    Reading Comprehension and Reading Experience Aid Vocabulary
    Development," *Journal of Learning Disabilities* 44, no. 5 (2011): 431-43,
    https://doi.org/10.1177/0022219411410042.

26 "New Survey: Demand for "Uniquely Human Skills" Increases
    Even as Technology and Automation Replace Some Jobs,"
    Cengage, January 16, 2019, https://news.cengage.com/upskilling/
    new-survey-demand-for-uniquely-human-skills-increases-even-as-
    technology-and-automation-replace-some-jobs/.

27 Ritchie J. Stuart, Timothy C. Bates, and Robert Plomin, "Does Learning to Read Improve Intelligence? A Longitudinal Multivariate Analysis in Identical Twins from Age 7 to 16," *Child Development* 86, no. 1 (2014): 23-36, https://doi.org/10.1111/cdev.12272.

28 Denise Rizzolo, et. al., "Stress Management Strategies for Students: The Immediate Effects of Yoga, Humor, and Reading on Stress," *Journal of College Teaching and Learning* 6, no. 8 (2009): 79-88, https://doi.org/10.19030/tlc.v6i8.1117.

29 Paul Heavenridge, "Why Read? Reason #7. The More One Reads, the Better Writer They Become," Literacy Works, published June 2, 2015, https://www.literacyworks.org/news/2015/6/2/why-read-reason-7-the-more-one-reads-the-better-writer-they-become#:~:text=The%20More%20One%20Reads%2C%20the%20Better%20Writer%20They%20Become.,-June%202%2C%202015&text=There%20are%20two%20ways%20to,lot%20and%20read%20a%20lot.&text="Reading%20exposes%20us%20to%20other,and%20helps%20us%20to%20improve.

30 "Character—What Is It and Why Is It important? by Michael Josephson," Josephson Institute's Exemplary Leadership & Business Ethics, accessed October 15, 2020, http://josephsononbusinessethics.com/2015/02/character-what-is-it-and-why-is-it-important/.

31 Roman Krznaric, "Six Habits of Highly Empathic People," *Greater Good Magazine*, published November 27, 2012, https://greatergood.berkeley.edu/article/item/six_habits_of_highly_empathic_people1.

32 Joel Garfinkle, "9 Tips for Improving Your Communications Skills," Garfinkle Executive Coaching, accessed October 15, 2020, https://garfinkleexecutivecoaching.com/articles/improve-your-communication-skills/9-tips-for-improving-your-communications-skills.

33 Daniela Fenker and Hartmut Schütze, "Learning By Surprise," Mind, published December 17, 2008, https://www.scientificamerican.com/article/learning-by-surprise/.

34 Philip Yaffe, "The 7% Rule: Fact, Fiction, or Misunderstanding," *Ubiquity* (2011): 1-5, https://doi.org/10.1145/2043155.2043156.

Made in the USA
Monee, IL
03 May 2024